# contents

Scripture taken from THE MESSAGE. Copyright © 1993, 1994, 1995, 1996, 2000, 2001, 2002. Used by permission of NavPress Publishing Group, PO Box 35001 Colorado Springs, CO 80935. www.messagebible.com

Every attempt has been made to gain the consent of parents and children for the publication of all the prayers and pictures.

quote on page four:
Robert Bensen: *Between the Dreaming and the Coming True:* San Francisco: HarperSanFrancisco, 1997, page 55 quoted in:
Michael Yaconelli: *Dangerous Wonder: the adventure of childlike faith:* NavPress, 1998, page 79

photographs on pages 17, 38, 50, 69 and 96 © Comstock
photographs on pages 12, 26, 32, 48, 64 and 111 © Stockdisc
photograph on page 54 used with permission

Children's Ministries Unit
101 Newington Causeway
London SE1 6BN
children@salvationarmy.org.uk

set in gill sans I lemonade I kids I tuesday
produced by CMU
design Nigel Brine
©copyright 2006
The Salvation Army UKT

# introduction

A book of prayers by children for children born out of The Salvation Army's International Year for Children and Youth.

Our thanks go to the 690 children from the length and breadth of the United Kingdom and from Ghana who have written their prayers. Even if you don't see your prayer in this book you know that God will have heard your prayer and seen your love.

For the adults to think about as they read the prayers:

*A four-year-old girl was overheard whispering into her newborn baby brother's ear, 'Baby,' she whispers, 'tell me what God sounds like. I am starting to forget.'*

This book comes with the hope that you may hear the whisper of God's voice through the prayers of his children.

As you have bought this book you have also contributed to Salvation Army projects seeking to bring love and hope to children round the world.

Such projects include those in Mozambique which ensure that children who have suffered the trauma of losing parents as a result of HIV/Aids will receive psychological support from a network of trained volunteers who will also place them within families in their own community; a community school project in Zambia will also benefit from the purchase of this prayer book.

By the end of this decade 30 million children around the world will be without parents. The Salvation Army, with your help, is enabling communities to care for some of these millions of children through holistic psychological, social and spiritual support programmes. Children are being supported and empowered to reach their full potential through pioneering initiatives but most importantly, because of the love they are receiving from their communities who have now committed to care for them. Education, health, nutrition and play are just a few of the vital ingredients to 'growing' these children into loving and independent adults. Thanks for helping us make a difference to their lives.

For more information about the projects please visit www.salvationarmy.org.uk/internationaldevelopment (the HIV/Aids and Sponsorship links)

so, let the prayers begin!

# foreword

Jesus said lots of exciting things about children but the best thing he said was, 'Let the children come to me!'

Prayer lets us come to God in a very special way. We can tell him how great he is! We can tell him when we are happy, hurt or sad and he is always there when we are scared and alone. As long as we pray with our heart and in an honest way, God is listening.

Sometimes he laughs with us, and sometimes he cries with us. He often says thank you back. He might say, 'Yes', 'No' or 'Wait a bit', but Jesus always hears and answers our prayers.

As you read this book and hear the prayers of other children, try and also pray the same prayers and hear the voice of Jesus in response.

A special donation from the sale of these books is going to help children all over the world who have less fortunate lives than some of us. Thank you for your part in changing their lives.

Blessings

Duncan Parker
Director of International
Development (UK) Salvation Army

When I was young I loved it when my friends asked, 'Do you want to play?' I now love hearing kids say, 'God, I want to pray!' Prayer is about being real with God, telling him when we are happy, excited, sad, scared or unhappy and it is about listening to what he wants to say to us.

I think this book is amazing because I believe that the openness and honesty of the prayers truly honours God and shows what Jesus meant when he said, 'I assure you that unless you change and become like children, you will never enter the Kingdom of heaven.'

Thanks for playing, and praying, your part in helping to change the lives of other children round the world.

God Bless

Roger

Major Roger Batt
Territorial Children's Ministries Unit
The Salvation Army

5

# The Lord is Here

Jesus you gave your life for me
For all the world
And that's easy to see

Lord oh God you made it true
Now all our lives
Are open to you

Salvation, salvation you helped us all
To read God's word
And spread through all

The Lord is here, the Lord is here
He'll comfort you
Far or near

So children laugh and children sing
The Lord is here
With peace he shall bring

Mary Jane age 9

dear
god

7

**God—you're my God! I can't get enough of you!**

Psalm 63:1

Dear God,

No matter how we treat you. No matter who we are. You Love us all the same and that's what matters most

Toni-Anne age 11

Hey God, just havin fun
with friinds, a short txt
to say How Gr8 u r!

Hey God, just been
thinking how much
u lov me and
how u sent your
Son 4 me how
cool!

Hey God, wat u
up 2? thanks 4
being there with
me 2day, talk
latr!

Hey God, Had a
Fall-out with
friends but it
all cool now I
said sorry glad
your there 4 me

Fiona age11

Dear God

Thank you God for all your wonderful creations and the many different animals that we have. We give thanks for all our food so that we may grow up big, strong and healthy. We hope that you will help and look after all the people who do not have as much as we do, and give them their hopes and dreams. In Jesus' name.
Amen.

Great

Omnipotent

dad

Yahweh

Order

Understanding

Awesome

Real

Everywhere

Amy age 8

Amy age 9

Dear Lord
Thankyou, for all the Beautiful days
you have given to us. And I pray that we will
enjoy this one. Thankyou for each Sunday
when we come to church and enjoy worshipping you.

AMEN

Gareth age 8

Thank you that
wherever I go you will
be right by my side to
guide me through
day and night.

God you're so great
because you love
and care for us.

Matthew age 8

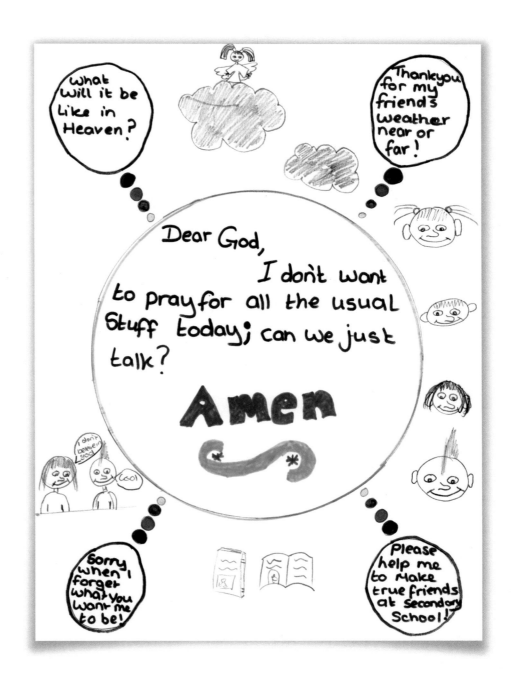

Jessica age 9

God you are grat ~~below~~
because you made the world.

Amen

by SARAh
Age 8

thank
you
prayers

**We thank you, God, we
thank you — your Name
is our favourite word;
your mighty works are
all we talk about.**

Psalm 75:1

**From the bottom of my
heart I thank you, dear
Lord;
I've never kept secret
what you're up to.
You've always been
great toward me—
what love!**

Psalm 86:12,13

Dear God,

Thank you for your
 preshus love and the
 world. Our men.
Oh and I couldn't forget
our mummys and daddys.

George age 6

Dear God,

Thank you for everything you
 have made
 for the bright sun
 for my fluffy bunny rabit
for the blue and green world
 for the different countries.
 Aarmen

Joshua age 8

Dear Jesus,

Thank you for
 The sun that shines,
 The birds that fly
 The rain that falls,
And the food we have.
 But most of all
 Thank you for living
 In a country
 Where I can enjoy them all
 And in freedom. We hope that
One day with your help
Everyone can live in peace
And freedom all over the world.
Amen.

Thomas age 9

17

Dear God,

Time
homes
animals
Nutrition
Kindness

You
Organs/veins and our heart.
Unconditional love

Grandparents
Overwhelming forgiveness
determination

Friends and family
Our awsome world.
royal family - God
                    Jesus
              Hdy Spirit

Hayden age 11

The morning mist, the starry skies
Soft fluffy ice-cream, hot steak and kidney pies
The snow peaked hills and bluebell-filled glens
Fat pot-bellied pigs and brown speckled hens
That big warm blanket that comforts me when I'm unwell
My Nan's love-filled hugs with that special Nan smell
My teacher, my friends, my Mum and Dad
My cute little sister, even my brother and he drives me mad
All of these things are special to me
These are your gifts and you give them with no fee
I'm thankful to someone, can you guess who?
That's right you've guessed it God....
I'm thankful to you.
Amen

Jordan age 11

Lord, Thank you for being there when I needed you the most and being there as a good friend to talk to in sad times in my life. Thank you for my family who supported me as I became a junior soldier to find out about you. Lord thank you for loving me and may I hope you love me forever.
Lord you're so great.
Love

Bethan age 9

Dear Lord,

We thank you that you love us all so much
That you hold the whole world in your hands.
We thank you that you gave us your Son to save us
From this sin soaked earth.

Amen

Abigail age 7

picture, Rebecca age 12

Dear God
Thank you for your help and love

Lewis age 9

Dear God
thank you God for makeing us with
love and happyhes and strenth   Armen.

Ailsa age 6

Prayer of Life

Thank you God for the life you have given me.
Thank you God for the air that I breathe.
God bless my family who love and care for me each day.
Thank you God for all the animals of the world and the
flowers that grow.
God bless all the people of the world.
Thank you God for giving us
      LIFE.

Holly age 11

Dear Lord Jesus

Thank you Lord for Playstations and
playing games at the park.
Thank you Lord for earthworms and
campfires in the dark.

Thank you Lord for Sleepovers that
could go on all night.
Thank you Lord for chocolate biscuits
when I take a bite.

Thank you Lord for football and
bicycles going wild.
Thank you Lord for making me and that
I am your child.
Amen

James age 10

picture, Erin age 6

Our father,
Thank you for helping us to
understand your ways.
We, as your people, want to
share your message but we know
we are useless without your help.
Help us to continue to follow you.
Amen

Angela age 10

Dear God, Thank-you for the wonderful world you gave us. It couldn't be any better.
Thank you for guiding me the right way to your love. Amen

Chloe

Dear Lord,
Thank you for
forgiving us and
dying for us. They
were very sorry that
you did but you
saved our lives.

Shelby age 8

Dear Jesus,

Thank you for being put to
death on a cross to save
my sins. You didn't have to
do it but you did to show
that you loved and cared
about me. Now all of my
sins are forgiven by you
when I say sorry to you.
You are the greatest.
Thank you Jesus. Amen

Chloe age 12


picture, Jamie age 8

God you are the greatest. You created the world and everything in it. You made each and every living thing beautiful and made sure they stay alive for as long as possible. Although some children round the world might not have homes we should be grateful for having what we have got especially a home. We thank you for our friends and family who care for us throughout whatever. We also thank you for pets and animals that we love to care for. Thank you for an education so we can learn about everything we need to at school. What I'm trying to say is you are so great infact your THE GREATEST.

Amen.

Me

Friends

family + Pet

Me

SCHOOL

Dear God

thank you for all the
nice things that
you have gave
to me this week
and I just want
to pray that
you gave such
good tings

forever,

In Jesus Powaful
name
Amen

Bethia age 6¾

Dear God
Thank you for the world.
Thank you for families that love each other.
Thank you God for special people
Thank you God for making me
Thank you God for looking over my family and friends.
Thank you for The Salvation Army and the people that run it.

Carrin age 9

Dear Jesus,

Thank you for outside where I
can play and for my watering
can to water the flowers.
Thank you for nursery school
and for my teachers who
teach me songs and play with
me. God bless mummy, God bless
daddy and God bless Samuel.

Amen

PS Please make Uncle Dave's
knee better

Marcia age 3

thank you em
for helicopters and
planes because they
help to rescue people
when they are lost amen

callum 5

Dear God

Thank you for all the chocalate.
Thank you for Buble gum.
Thank you for breack off school
so we can mess about.
Thank you for my mum and dad.
A.men

chocalate bar

Daniel age 9

thanks
for
creation

29

**God, brilliant Lord,**
**yours is a household name.**

**Nursing infants gurgle**
**choruses about you;**
**toddlers shout the songs**
**That drown out enemy talk,**
**and silence atheist babble.**

**I look up at your macro-skies,**
**dark and enormous,**
**your handmade sky-jewelry,**
**Moon and stars mounted in**
**their settings.**
**Then I look at my micro-self**
**and wonder,**
**Why do you bother with us?**
**Why take a second look our**
**way?**

Psalm 8:1-3

Dear God,
We thank you for creation, for all the beautiful views and seas. You created us to look after your world. You created the sun, moon, earth, sky, night and day. We thank you for the creation and we promise to help look after all you have created.
Amen

Elizabeth age 12

Dear God
Thank you for the lovely world, thank you for the sun that
gives us light, thank you for all the things around us. Amen

Sophie age 7

Dear God

Thank you for the lion's roar,
Thank you for ever more,
Thank you for the bleat of a new born lamb,
Thank you for your wonderful plan.

Thank you for the stars that sparkle,
Thank you for the sky so blue,
Thank you for your wonderful creation,
And all things you make new.

Help me to appreciate beauty,
And take care of all you have made,
To remind me of your greatness,
And your love that will not fade!

Amen

Maddie age 8

Dear God

Thank you for making the trees and flowers

they make our world beautiful and help our

world to survive for men.

Lewis age 6

Dear Lord,
Thank you for this wonderful
world you made for us and
thank you for creating all the
special things you made for
us to use in our needs.

Chloe age 9

thank you for the
worLd. And for the
water, thank you for
my friends, and people. please help
me to look after my pets.

Amen

Ieuan age 9

thanks for pets and animals

What a wildly wonderful world, God!
    You made it all, with Wisdom at your side,
    made earth overflow with your wonderful creations.
Oh, look — the deep, wide sea,
    brimming with fish past counting,
    sardines and sharks and salmon.
Ships plough those waters,
    and Leviathan, your pet dragon, romps in them.
All the creatures look expectantly to you
    to give them their meals on time.
You come, and they gather around;
    you open your hand and they eat from it.

Psalm 104: 24-28

Thank you for
creating our world
and for making the
shells on snails and for
making the wings on
butterflies and for the
animals that you made
and for all the plants.

Thank you. Amen

Charlotte age 9

my dog by Nigel age 44 ¼

Dear God,

Thank you for all the animals. Thank you for my hamster Harry.
Please don't let people be bad to animals. Watch over them.

Rhegan age 6

Dear God thank for PiGEons and food.

Oliver age 9

Dear Father,
Thank you for creating so many animals.
They are all different in their own ways.
There are different pets that we can have for ourselves.
Please help us to be kind to every type of animal.
Thank you Lord
AMEN

Gemma age 7

Dear Jesus,

Thank you for my horses and my duck
Daphne. You are my helper and my
friend.
Love from Olivia. Amen

age 7

Thankyou God that you saved all the animals and Noahs family from the flood so that we could live.
Thankyou that you sent the rainbow to show you will never flood the world again.

Amen

Kate

Kate age 11

Dear God, I thank you for the animals and the deers and the crocodiles. Thank you God for looking after me.
Amen

Joshua age 4

Father God,

Thankyou for all the animals you created. from the biggest elephant to the smallest spider
Thankyou that we can have pets to look after.
We know there are some people who are cruel to your creatures. Help us to protect them and look after and love them as you do for us.
    Amen.

Abbi age 9

# sporty prayers

God, investigate my life; get all the facts firsthand.
  I'm an open book to you;
      even from a distance, you know what I'm thinking.
  You know when I leave and when I get back;
      I'm never out of your sight...
      I look behind me and you're there,
      then up ahead and you're there, too —
      your reassuring presence, coming and going.
  This is too much, too wonderful —
      I can't take it all in!

Psalm 139: 1-3,5-6

Thank you for sport and leisure. Thank you for keeping us fit and healthy. Thank you for the people who own the sport equipment, and places to keep us fit so we can have fun and meet other people.  Amen

Rachel  9

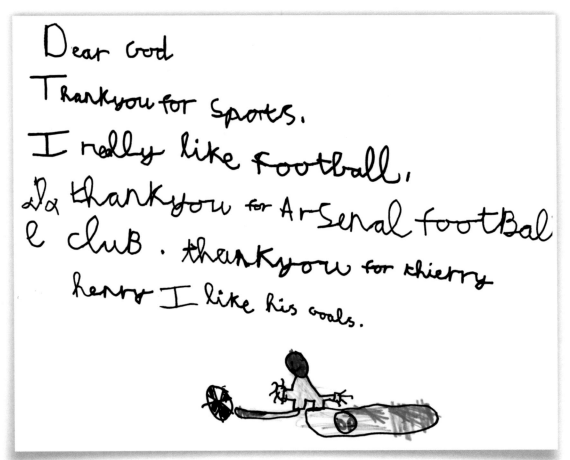

Dear God
Thankyou for sports.
I really like football,
Da thankyou for Arsenal footBall cluB. thankyou for thierry henry I like his goals.

Kyle age 7

Thank you Lord for sports. What would I do with out football, rugby, cricket and lots more. There is never a boring game because God you make it brill.

Luke age 9

Dear Lord, thank you for the development of english sports. Please help the resources we have here get over into the countries that don't have what we have. AMEN

James age 11

Thank you for my strong bones that help me when I play sport, and for patience when I am playing as part of a team.

Anon

Dear God
Please help me play football because the other boys are too fast for me
Please help me to run fast. Amen    Isaac age 4

please
prayers

45

**Open your ears, God, to my prayer; don't pretend you don't hear me knocking. Come close and whisper your answer. I really need you.**

Psalm 55:1-2

'A private prayer between me and God about fixing a robot' David  age 7

Dear God
Please keep everybody safe, everybody happy,
give everybody a talent,
help everybody in school,
help everyone that is working,
help everybody at home and out and about.

Lewis age 10

Dear God,

Please take care of
all my friends at
playgroup and their
families. I like to
play in the garden.
Thank you for the
sunshine and rain
that makes the
flowers grow.

Michael age 4

Dear God

Please help people not to smoke.
Please help us to take care of
ourselves.
Amen

Amalie age 6

Dear God,

Please can you give Tots's
kittens a safe, gentle home.
They've nearly been alive for
6 days, because they were
born in the night. My mum
says we have to get rid of
them in 8 weeks but I want
to get rid of them in 12
weeks.
Thank-you,
Amen

Nancy age 8

Dear Lord, help us Lord

help us to live a helpful life
help us to conquer over evil strife
help us to live the truth
help us to confess the lies

Please help me to live for you
Please be with me in all I do
Sit beside me as I learn
Please be my greatest teacher
You taught me, me

Betsy age 9

Dear God, please be with the
new Pope so he can have a
good time and look after
people. Please let him have a
nice time and don't let him get
shot like John Paul the II.
Please look after him. Amen

Adam age 11

sorry
prayers

Generous in love — God, give grace!
Huge in mercy — wipe out my bad record.
 Scrub away my guilt,
      soak out my sins in your laundry.
 I know how bad I've been;
      my sins are staring me down.

Psalm 51:1-3

Dear God,
You brought my life
together. You love me and I
know you always will because
I love you. Thank you for family
and friends, mums and dads, houses
and school, and most important
Jesus. Sorry for all my mistakes
and all things that I have
done wrong. Amen

Sorry Jesus

my Family

School

Harriet age 7

Oh my God, because you are so good I
am very sorry for what I have done so
please take care of me every day. Amen

Mathew age 8

Dear God,
Sorry for not
listening
when I have
been naughty.
Amen

Connor age 6

54

i love
you

God, my shepherd! I don't need a thing.
  You have bedded me down in lush meadows,
    you find me quiet pools to drink from.
True to your word,
    you let me catch my breath
    and send me in the right direction.

Even when the way goes through
    Death Valley,
  I'm not afraid
    when you walk at my side.
Your trusty shepherd's crook
    makes me feel secure.

You serve me a six-course dinner
    right in front of my enemies.
You revive my drooping head;
    my cup brims with blessing.

Your beauty and love chase after me
    every day of my life.
I'm back home in the house of God
    for the rest of my life.

Psalm 23

picture, Imogen age 4

Jesus oh Jesus, you died for me
Jesus oh Jesus how can it be

Lord oh Lord I love you so
Lord oh Lord I hope you know

God oh God I pray to you
And hope that you will make them true

Catherine age 9

To God,
I love Jesus as
well as you and
look after
everyone in the
whole world.
Amen

Joshua age 5

Dear Lord
I pray that you will be with people
who maybe aren't as lucky as me.
Please be with everyone whoever
or wherever they are or who they
are. O Lord, we love you, we want
to love you. Thanks for all you do
and who you are.  Amen

*Rebecca age 9*

picture, Georgia

special
times

**Applause, everyone.**
**Bravo, bravissimo!**
**Shout God-songs at**
**the top of your lungs!**

**God Most High**
**is stunning**

Psalm 47:1,2a

Dear Lord.

Thank you for my family and
friends and pets. Thank you for
food and drink and for sports like
football and skateboarding.
Thank you for all different types
of weather especially snow. But
most of all thank you for dying on
the cross for our sins at Easter
which we will remember soon, for
sending us the holy spirit which
will stay with us forever.
Amen

Kelly-Marie age 11

Thank god for harvest for giving food and growing crops, Oh lord there are Some countries where there is not enough food to go around. Please help us to be generous thank you For sweets, crisps and healthy things too. But most of all thank you For our family's and Friends.

Amen

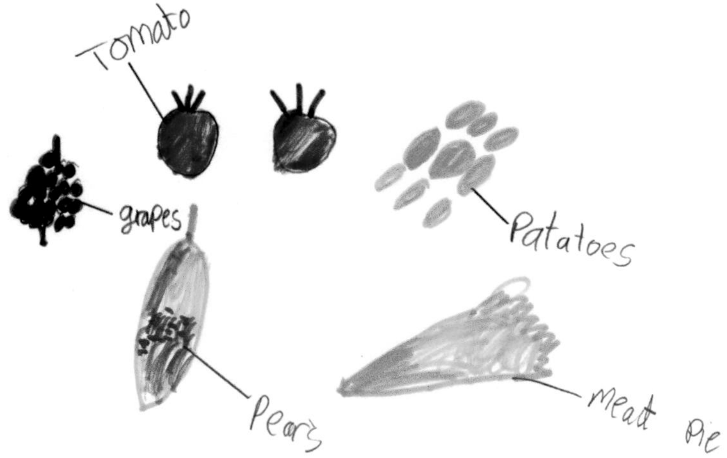

Tomato

grapes

Patatoes

Pears

meat pie

Rosie

Thank you for the food we like.
Sweets, crisps, chocolate
and chips.
But also thank you for
the healthy foods,
Rice, spaghetti, fruit
and vegetables.   Amen

Alice

'I don't do prayers'

Dear God,

I really don't know what to say today
I never think about what to pray
You already know what's in my head
You know how and what needs to be said
It's brill that Christmas is nearly here
Yet to me it's obvious and clear
You really are the coolest dude around
Although you could be cooler if there was snow on the ground!
Thank you for being Jesus's dad
'cos without him my life would be bad not glad
Thanks a bunch for helping when I hurt
Better go now, speak soon love Kurt
Amen

Kurt age 10

# family prayers

65

Like a baby content in its mother's arms,
my soul is a baby content.

Psalm 131:2

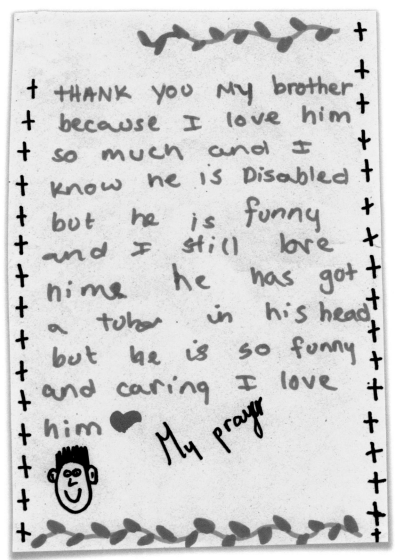

THANK you My brother because I love him so much and I know he is Disabled but he is funny and I still love nime he has got a tuba in his head but he is so funny and caring I love him ♥ My prayer

Coral age 10

Dear God
I miss grandad and I hope
that he is in
heaven with you
please look after him
for me
thank you
Amen

Tilly age 5

Dear God,

Please help us respect our families
even in the moodiest of times and
thank you for all the colours in the
rainbow and for putting them into
our lives otherwise it would be dull
and blank. Thank you for families
and siblings.

Sarah age 10

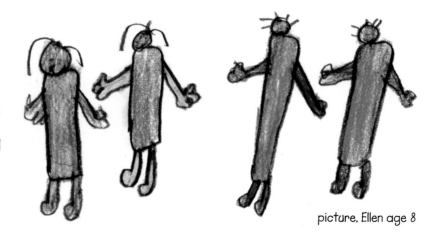

picture, Ellen age 8

Oh dear God, I thank you for protection you have given to my family. Oh God, help my family to live long on this earth and enable them to get money in a needed time and places. Lord, help them to get good jobs in future. I believe you really died for us and I hope you will forgive our sins when we ask. Please God, help my family to love and obey your words and commands. In Jesus' name have I prayed. Amen!!

Daniel age 12

Thank you for our friends and family, inside or upset. We thank you for these things.

Mark age 7

Dear God I love my mummy very much. She is very kind and helpful. Amen

Chloe age 6

Dear God,

Thank you for our loving parents which look after us and take care of us because they love us very much. Thank you God for creating me and my family that I love so much. I couldn't ask for a better family in the world. Amen

Hannah age 11

Dear God
Thank you for my
family that I live
with and I love.
Please help those
who don't have a
family to live with
or love. Please
give them a family.
Amen

*Niomie age 8*

# friends

God's love is meteoric,
    his loyalty astronomic,
His purpose titanic,
    his verdicts oceanic.
Yet in his largeness
    nothing gets lost;
Not a man, not a mouse,
    slips through the cracks.....

Keep on loving your friends;
    do your work in welcoming hearts.

Psalm 36:5,6,10

dear god.
thank you
for for
friends

Zoë age 4

Dear God,
Thank you that
my friends can
come to my
house and play
football. Thank
you God for my
football.
Amen

Nathan age 3

picture, Joseph age 4

Our dear Lord and Master. Saviour we thank you for all the things you
have done for us. Father, I pray committing my friends into your hands.
Lord I pray that you will protect them from evil and bless them in
everything they do. Lord I pray that you will open their mind in
everything they do. I pray that you will continue to bless them and
continue to take care of them. I pray that you will help their mothers
and fathers to pay their school fees. I pray that you will bless their
family. In Jesus' Name I pray. Amen

Gifty age 7

Dear God,
My friend was being bullied all the time but I
prayed about it and it stopped. Thank You God.
Amen x

Francesca age 11

Dear God,
I pray for giving me good friends. If I did not have any friends I would be unhappy.
They play with me. Friends are there if you are hurt. They come and help you. They are caring and helpful.
My family are like my friends, they are caring and concerned for me.
Dear Lord, be with all the people and children who feel they have no friends. Help them to know that you are their true friend.

Siôn age 10

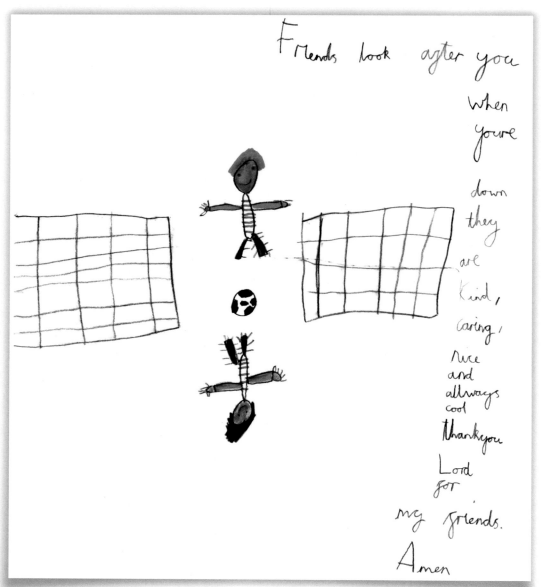

Friends look after you
when
you're

down they
are
kind,
caring,
nice
and
allways
cool
Thankyou
Lord
for
my friends.
Amen

Harry age 8

# school prayers

Show me how you work, GOD;
School me in your ways.
Take me by the hand;
Lead me down the path of truth.
You are my Saviour, aren't you?

Psalm 25:4,5

Dear God
help my teachers so they can get
to know you

Josh age 8

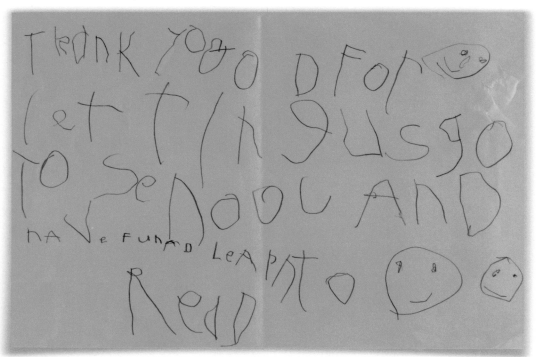

Peter age 5

Dear Lord,
Thank you for all the help you give me. I am lucky that I can come to you at any time I have problems with my school work but I am learning to trust you more to help me.

Scott

Dear Lord,
Please help us at school. When we find our lessons hard or we are being bullied, help us to remember to pray for help. If someone is trying to make us do something that we know is wrong let us say no. Thank you for our teachers and all the school equipment we have. Thank you for our school friends and all the games and books. Please help us to be good at school and to do well at our work. Amen

Sophie age 10

Dear God,

Thank you for letting me go to school.
Thank you for my friends who play with me.
Thank you for the teachers who help us to learn.
Thank you for assemblies where we pray.
Thank you for the dinner ladies who look after us at dinner time.
Amen

Millicent age 6

Kindness

love

Dear God

Thank-you for rainbows, I love there pretty colours. Please help me to let your love shine through me, so I can make rainbows at my school

Amen

PEACE

Helpfulness

Happieness

Phoebe age 9

# healing prayers

**Is anyone crying for help?**
**God is listening,**
**ready to rescue you.**

Psalm 34:17

I pray committing the sick into your mighty hands, Father for we know that you are the only person who can heal the sick and that with you all things are possible so, Father at this moment I commit the sick in the world into your hands. Father, heal them in spirit... Bless them in whatever they do and when they get their recovering we shall give praise and honour and glorify your holy name. This and many blessings we have asked through your son who died for our sins in Jesus' name. AMEN

Bernice age 12

Lord,
Help the people all
over the world who
are injured, hurt or
anything else. Help
the people who are
old and weak. Help
the people who
help us.
Amen

Bethany age 9

Dear Lord Jesus
Please bless the old people that are sick and help them to get better. Help the nurses and doctors to give them the right medicine.
Please take care of the people that have not got any homes and that live on the streets. Please bless the children that have not got mummies.
Thank you that I have a mummy.
Thank you that I am not sick.
   Thank you that I am not sitting in the cold.
   Thank you that I have food to eat every breakfast, lunch and supper time.
   Thank you for all these things.
Amen

Rebecca age 7

Dear Lord
Please Help people in bad times
and keep sick people in your
hands. AMEN

Jordan age 7

Dear God
When my
frinds are
Poorly
Please
make
them better
Amen

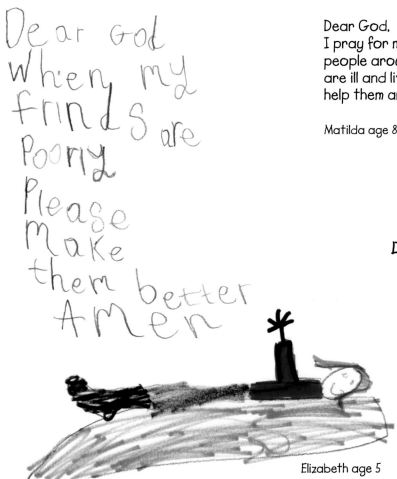

Elizabeth age 5

Dear God,
I pray for my grandma in heaven and all of the people around me. I also pray for people that are ill and live on the streets in Africa. Please help them and I thank you for my health. Amen.

Matilda age 8

Dear Lord,
I pray for the people who are sick. I pray that you will help them to get better. Amen

Deborah age 6

Dear God

thank you for helping me feel
better when I am sick even
though its Mummy who
empties the bucket

Amen

Nathan age 7

church
prayers

How wonderful, how beautiful,
when brothers and sisters get along!
    It's like costly anointing oil
        flowing down head and beard,
    Flowing down Aaron's beard,
        flowing down the collar of his priestly robes.

Psalm 133: 1-2

Thank you Lord for Sunday school. I like Sunday school. It is good fun and I learn about you. Thank you Lord for friends.

Aran age 7

Dear God,
Thank you for my Salvation Army and for all the people who make it so special. Help our church to be a happy and caring and loving place.
Amen

Luke age 7
Luke's picture is on page 112

my leaders

Audra  evelyn  marion  colin

Aynslie age 9

Dear Father in heaven
Please look after all my Sunday school
leaders and take care of them as they get
older. I thank them for doing everything for
us and taking care of us.

The Sunday school leaders are very
lovable and care for other people. I like being
in our groups because it's very fun. We get to
make lots of fun stuff. Take care of them
please. Amen

Dear God,
Thank you for my corps and thank you
for our officers who have only been
here since last June. Be with people
who are less fortunate than us. Thank
you for the world that you made and
that you made it with amazing things.
And be with me as I am doing my Sats in
May and I hope that it's not on the
24th as that's my birthday.

Josh age 10

# community prayers

93

God, mark us with grace and blessing! Smile!
The whole country will see how you work,
all the godless nations see how you save.
God! Let people thank and enjoy you.
Let all people thank and enjoy you.

Psalm 67:1,2

Dear God,
Please look after the people who
aren't as fortunate as we are.
Please look after the animals and
plants. Thank you for food and
water. Please help the victims of
war and fights. Please help the
people who live on the streets.
Please help people in jail. Please
help everyone to see that you are
the one who looks after us.
Amen

Peter age 9

Dear God,
I pray that you will help anybody, anywhere, whatever people
are doing that you will bless them. I pray this all in your holy and
awesome name. Amen

Sarah age 10

Dear God,

Thank you for the Scottish
government and all the decisions
they make for children. Help them
to make a better Scotland.
Amen

Brooke age 7

95

Dear Lord God,

Thank you for the Community I live in.
Please help the people in it that are poorly to get better
and people that have great health to give money to the
poor that have no food.
Please help people to put their rubbish in the bin so that no
one has to pick up rubbish that is not their own.
Please help people to find different ways rather than using
smoke, steam and petrol, like using your bike so not to break
the ozone layer and keep the world clean.
Thank you God for people like the police, ambulance people,
firemen, postmen, rubbish men, paper boys and everyone that
cares for us. Please look after them as they do their jobs.
Please help our teachers to be safe and to teach us things
for our lives in the future.
Thank you God for the wonderful world I live in. Amen

Katie age 7

# children around the world

**God, brilliant Lord,
your name echoes around the world.**

Psalm 8:9

Dear Jesus,
Please look after the poorly children and children who haven't got toys. Amen

Jonah age 3

Dear God,
Please stand by
the children and
adults when
they have a
problem and help
them with their
problem.

Hannah age 9

Dear God Please help all the children like
you help me and also please give them
food and a warm bed to sleep in and
shoes for their feet. Amen

Tulasi age 8

Dear Lord

Thank you for all the food you give
us. We are lucky to have food and
warm clothes. Some children are
unlucky because they don't have
any food or anything but we are
very lucky. We hope they get
better soon and get new food
and water too. Amen

Amy age 8

picture, Tory age 10

Dear father God,
Please bless the children
in the world that are
less fortunde than me and
who do nod have a safe bed to
sleep in. Bless them father and let
them know that you care for them
with all your heart.

God is wonderful. He is with
us every day. He made all the
animals and
People in the world.
Isnt God wonderful? Amen.

by Lindsay

Lindsay age 6

Dear Lord,
Please help the sick, the dying, the poor and hungry. And the uneducated so they can go to school and learn the things we learn. And help the children of the world. Amen

Alison age 10

Dear Lord
Thank you for me and all the other children around the world. I pray for the people who don't have as much as me. Thank you Jesus for loving every children and adults. We also pray for the children who have lost their mums and dads in the tsunami. Please send someone to help them, Amen

Kirsty age 12

Dear Lord,
We pray for those in far-off lands who aren't well off as we are. May they know that you are with them. We pray that you'll be in the many different places where there is war. Please be with the families and friends of those people who have been killed. Amen

Alfred age 10

Dear God,
Please help the people where there is no water, food and shelter like the people on the comic relief film and the people struck by the big wave.
Yours sincerely

Kieran age 11

Dear God

Please help the children all around the world who are struggling to get food to eat, to get clean water and shelter to sleep in at night. I especially pray for the children who live in Indonesia who have just witnessed the tsunami and have no home to live in. Amen

picture, Chelsea age 12

Philip age 9

Dear god,
Thankyou for all the animals and espestrcially gini-pigs. Thank you for shools and the People who work in them. help People in the world who are sick and help hospitals to get better Tecknolagey, help The People who were in The sunami wave. and help the world to be a better Place

Amen

Rebecca age 9

hopes
and
dreams

Don't put your life in the hands of experts
    who know nothing of life, of salvation life.
Mere humans don't have what it takes;
    when they die, their projects die with them.
Instead, get help from the God of Jacob,
    put your hope in God and know real blessing!

Psalm 146:3-5

Joseph age 9

Dear God,

I hope that I will manage to live in
Australia and work in a zoo. Because
animals are the passion of my life
And I hope you will guide me there.
Amen

Sam age 11

Dear Lord please help everyone to fulfil
their hopes and dreams. I dream to be a
footballer for Arsenal football club.

But Lord help the people in Africa and in
poor places to get their dreams and
hopes. All they want is a healthy life and
to be loved.

And Lord help and let the churches and
Salvation Armys to fulfil their dreams and
help the poor. Amen

Shobi age 10

Dear God. My hopes and dreams are special, and God agrees with me. My hopes and dreams are different, from the person next to me. My hopes and dreams will make a difference, in the world around me. My hopes and dreams are special and God will encourage me. I may not be a nurse or a fireman too but whatever I do to help the world I do it by praising you.

TWISTER

Amen

Lauren age 11

When I grow up I would like to be a fireman.

# evening prayer

**At day's end I'm ready for sound sleep,**
**For you, God, have put my life back together.**

Psalm 4:8

Dear Lord,
Thank you for everything that
has happened to me today.
Please forgive me for anything
I have done wrong.
Please guard my family through
the night. Amen

Kristi age 11

Luke age 7